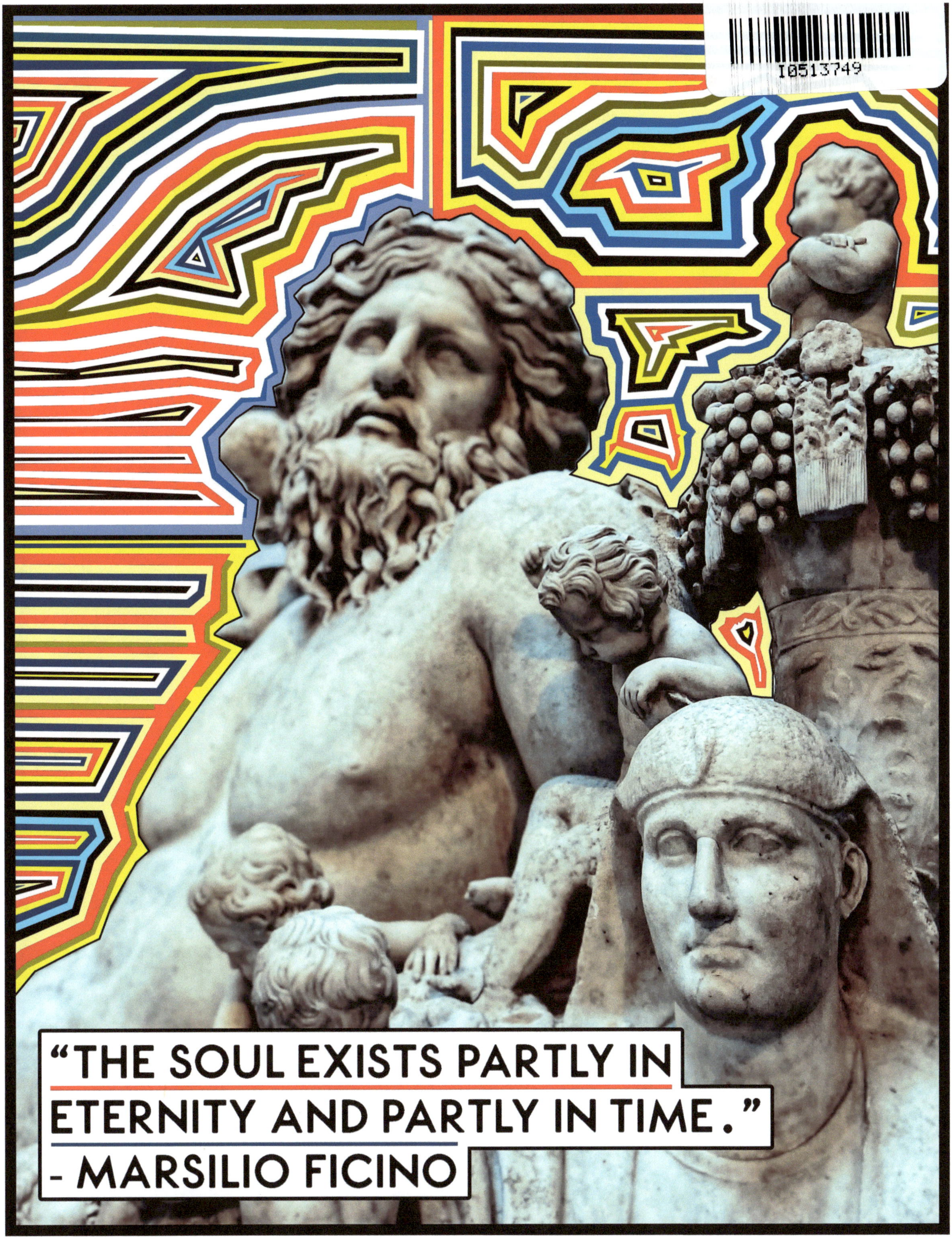
"THE SOUL EXISTS PARTLY IN ETERNITY AND PARTLY IN TIME."
- MARSILIO FICINO

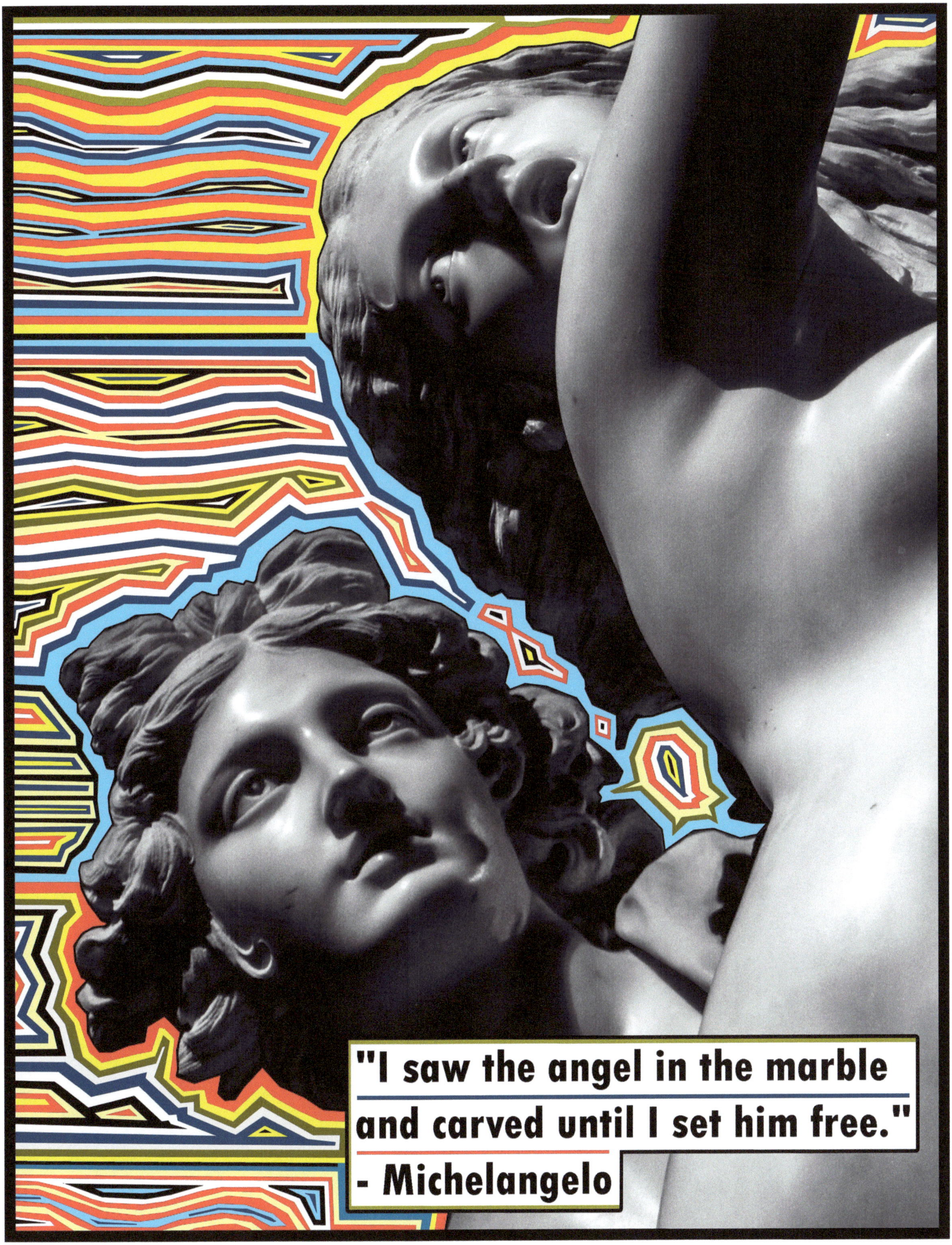
"I saw the angel in the marble
and carved until I set him free."
- Michelangelo

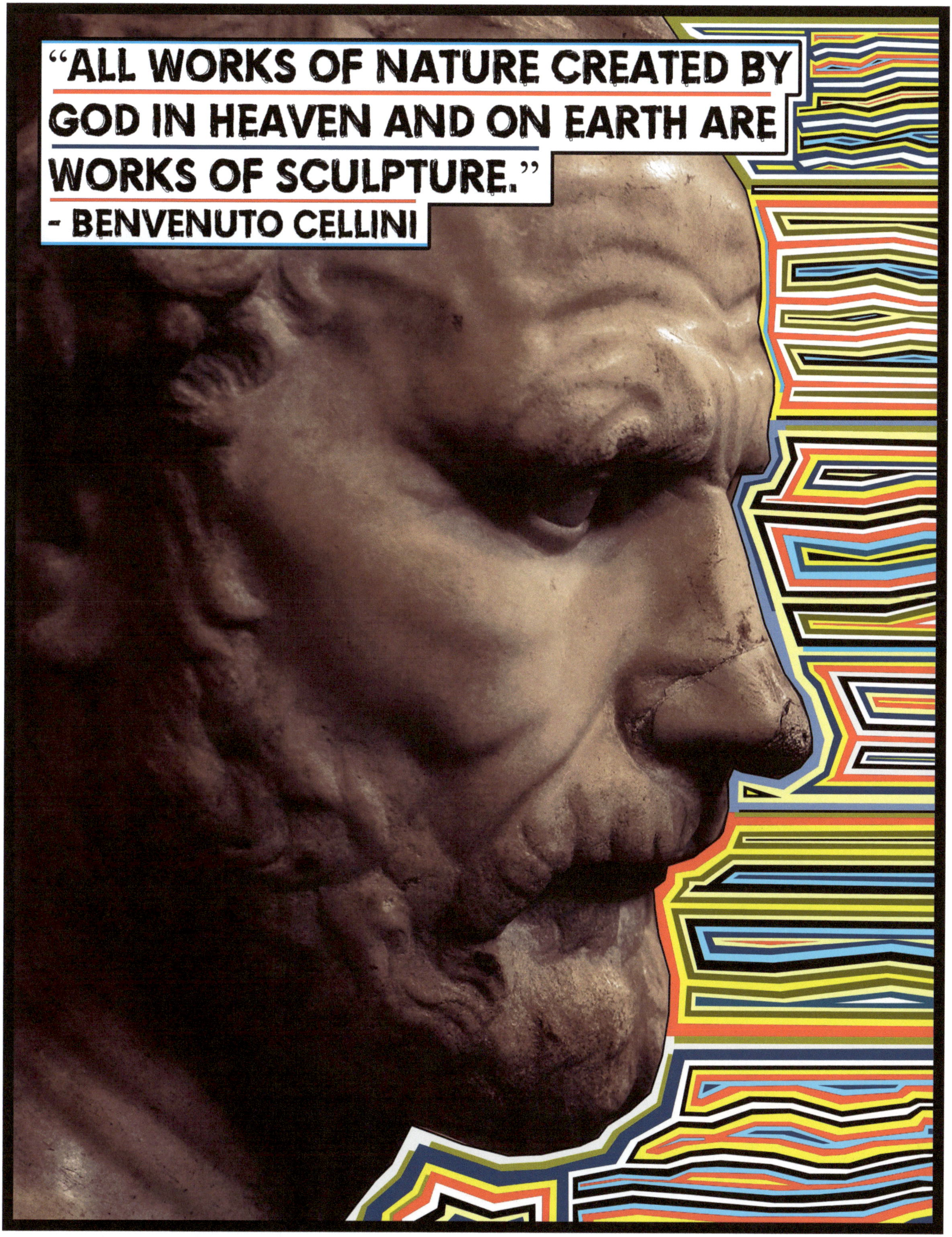
"ALL WORKS OF NATURE CREATED BY
GOD IN HEAVEN AND ON EARTH ARE
WORKS OF SCULPTURE."
- BENVENUTO CELLINI

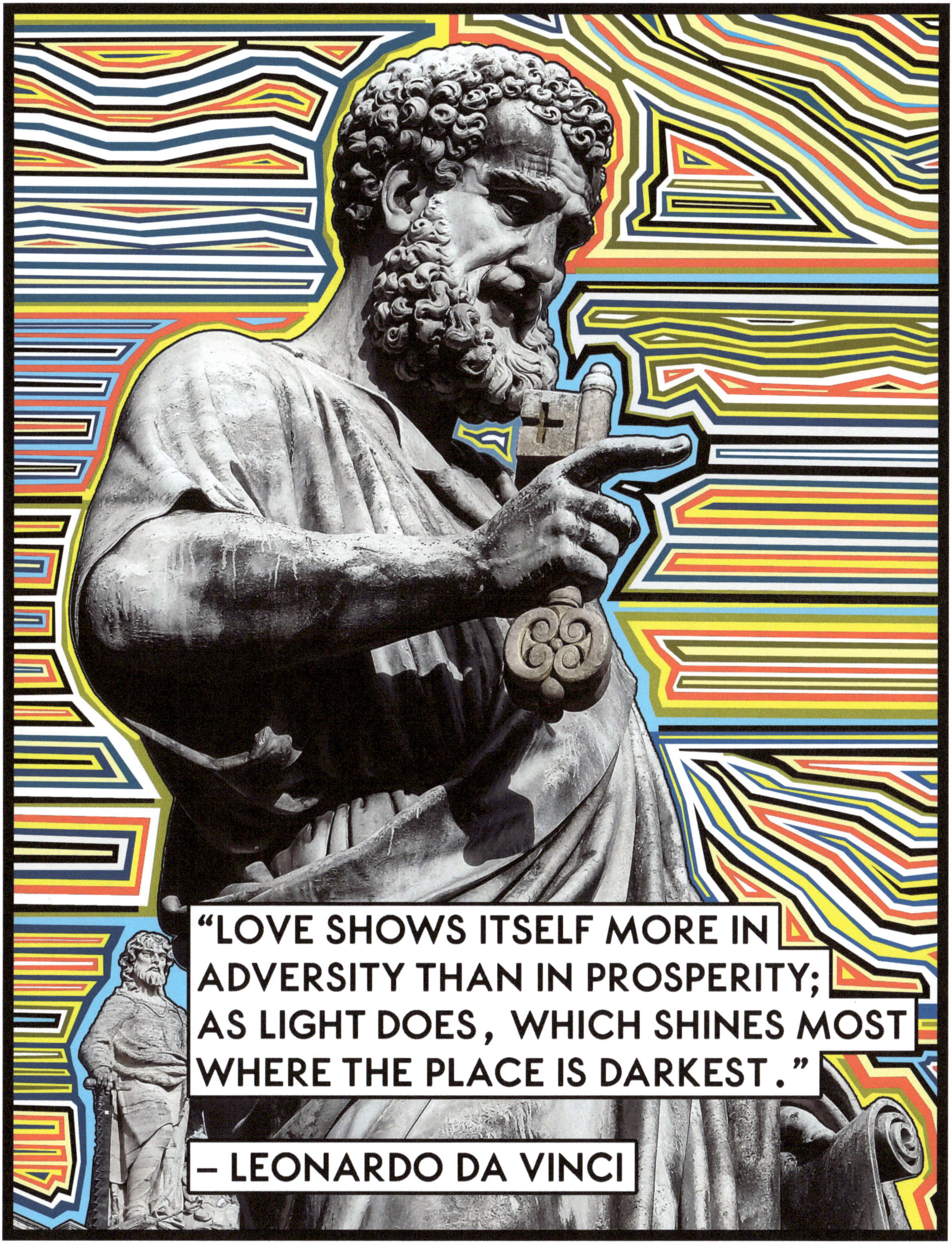
"LOVE SHOWS ITSELF MORE IN ADVERSITY THAN IN PROSPERITY; AS LIGHT DOES, WHICH SHINES MOST WHERE THE PLACE IS DARKEST."
– LEONARDO DA VINCI

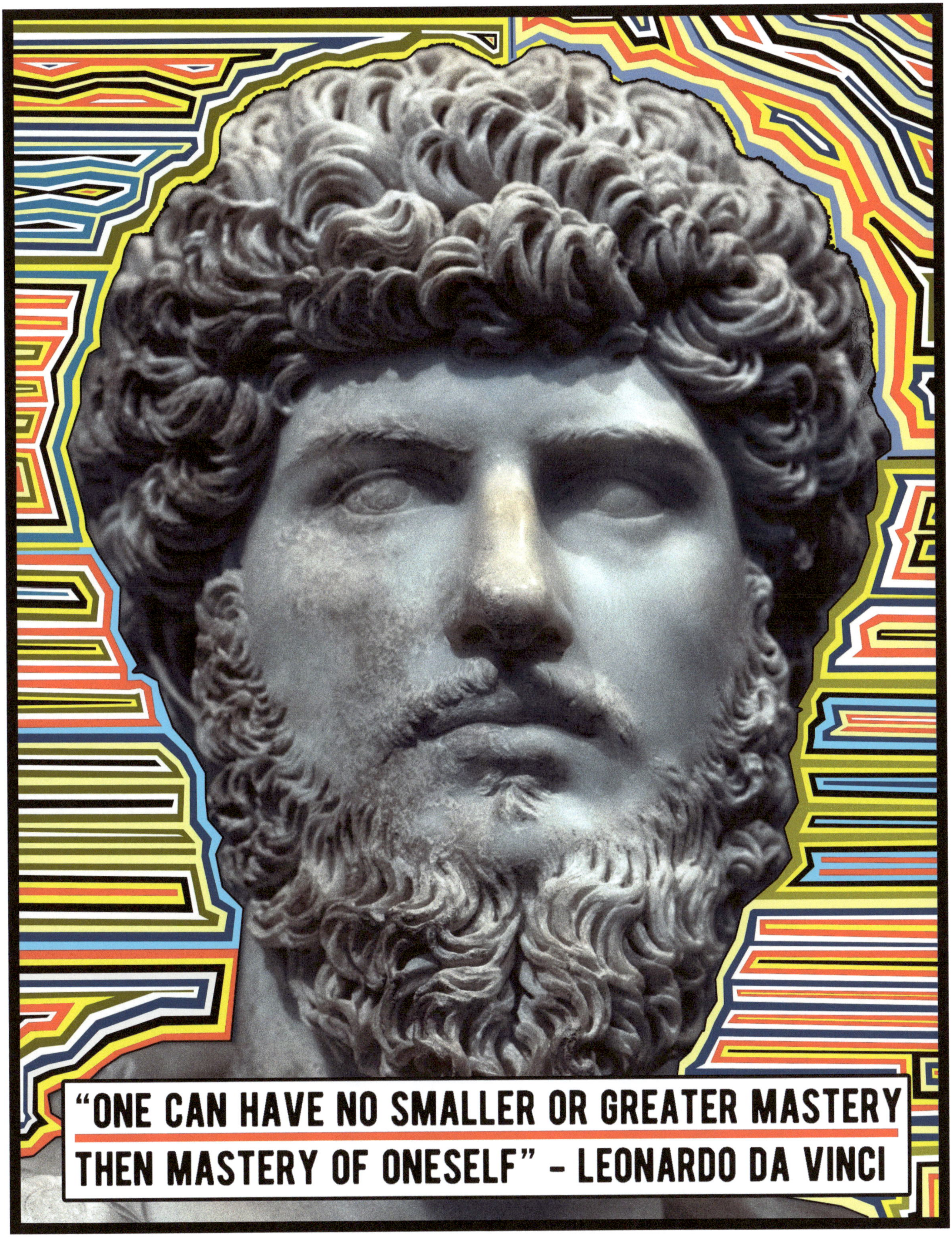
"ONE CAN HAVE NO SMALLER OR GREATER MASTERY
THEN MASTERY OF ONESELF" - LEONARDO DA VINCI

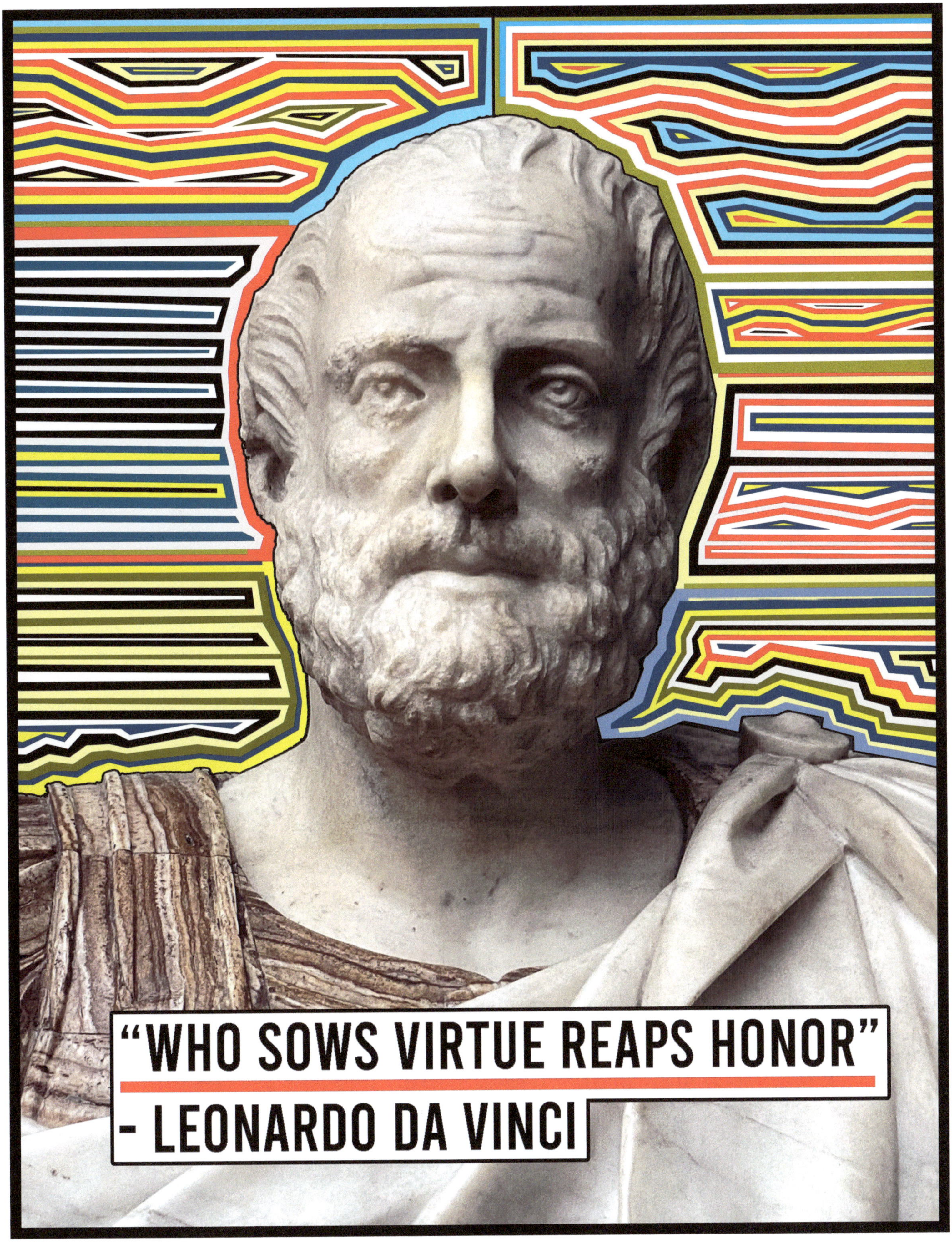
"WHO SOWS VIRTUE REAPS HONOR"
- LEONARDO DA VINCI

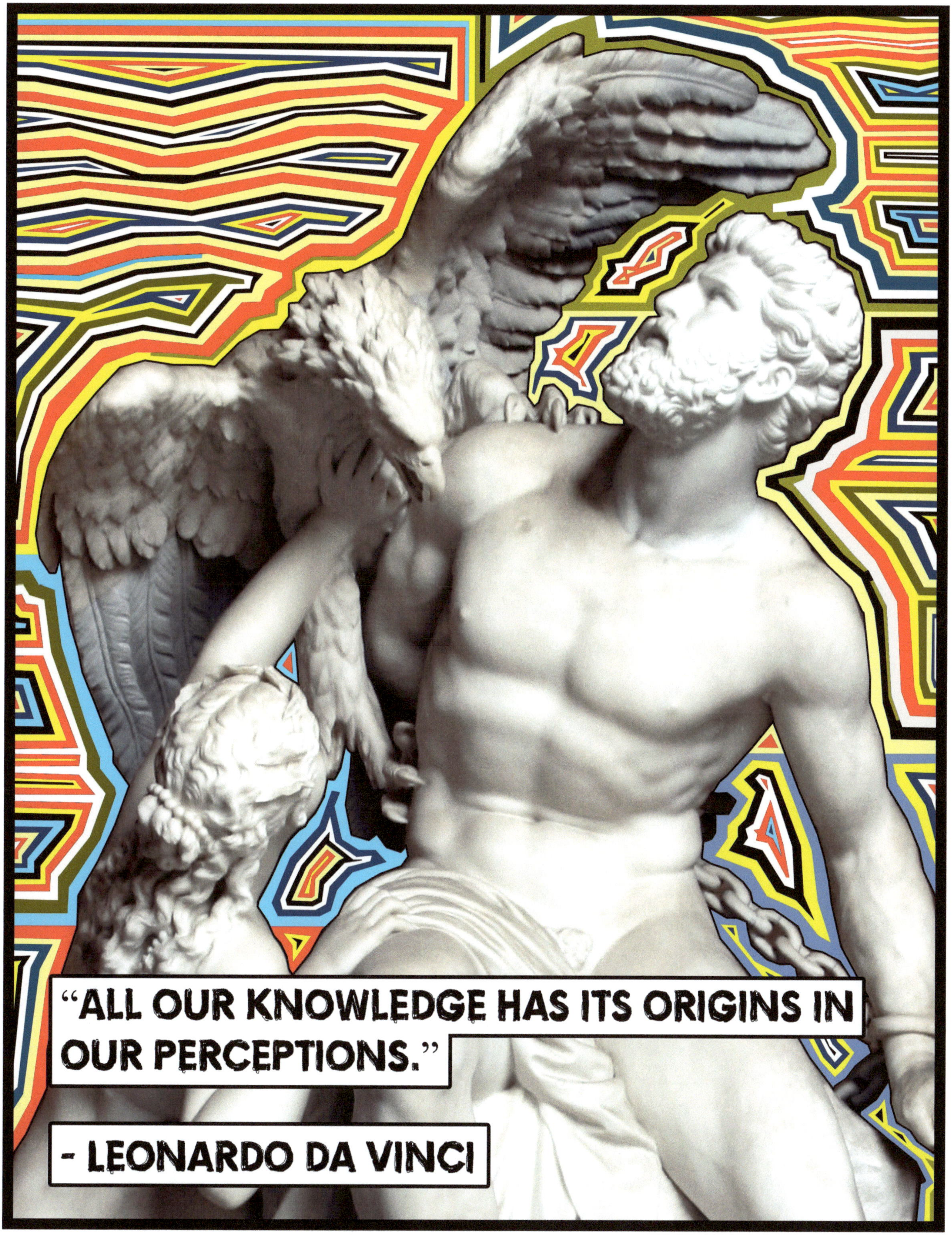
"ALL OUR KNOWLEDGE HAS ITS ORIGINS IN OUR PERCEPTIONS."
- LEONARDO DA VINCI

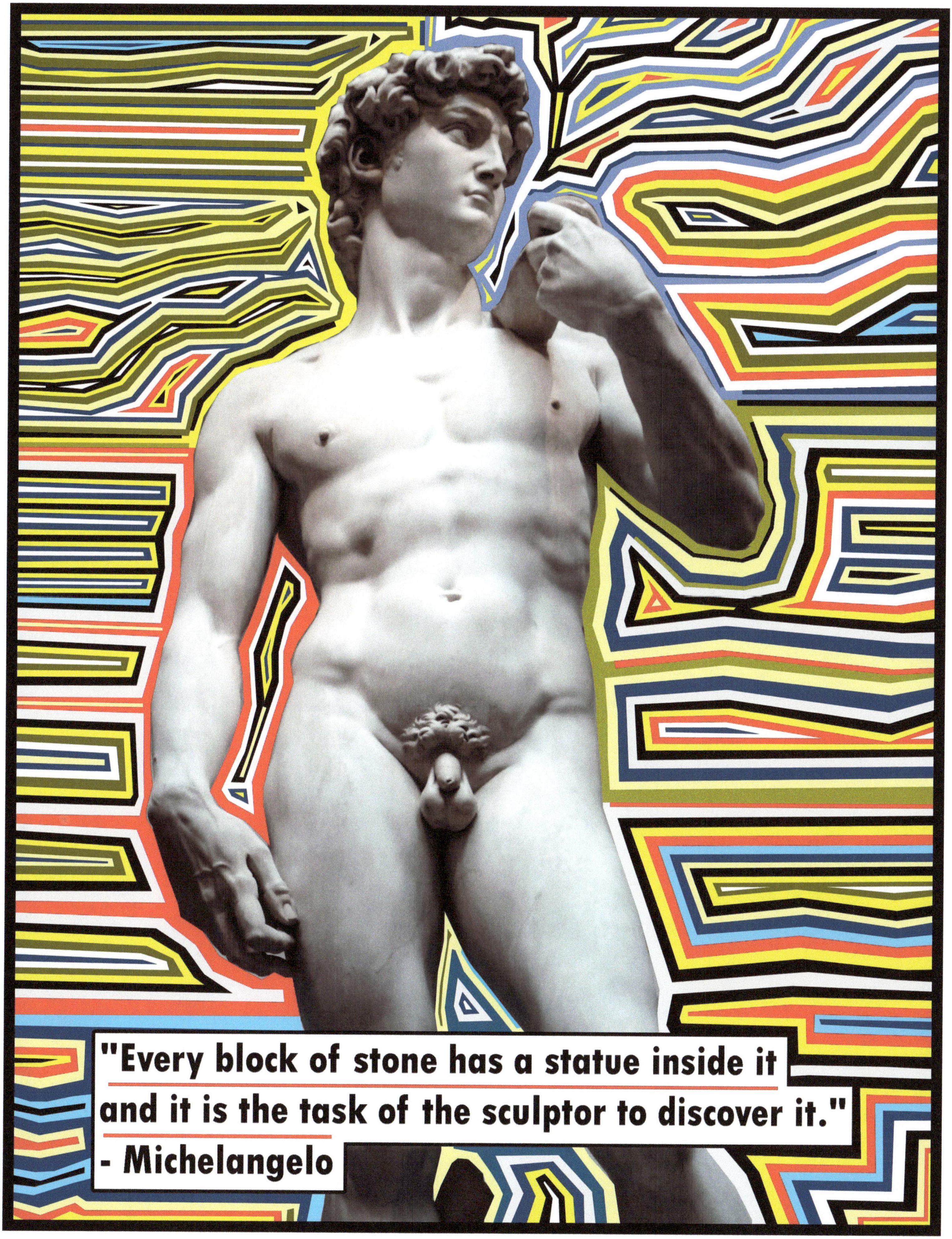
"Every block of stone has a statue inside it
and it is the task of the sculptor to discover it."
- Michelangelo

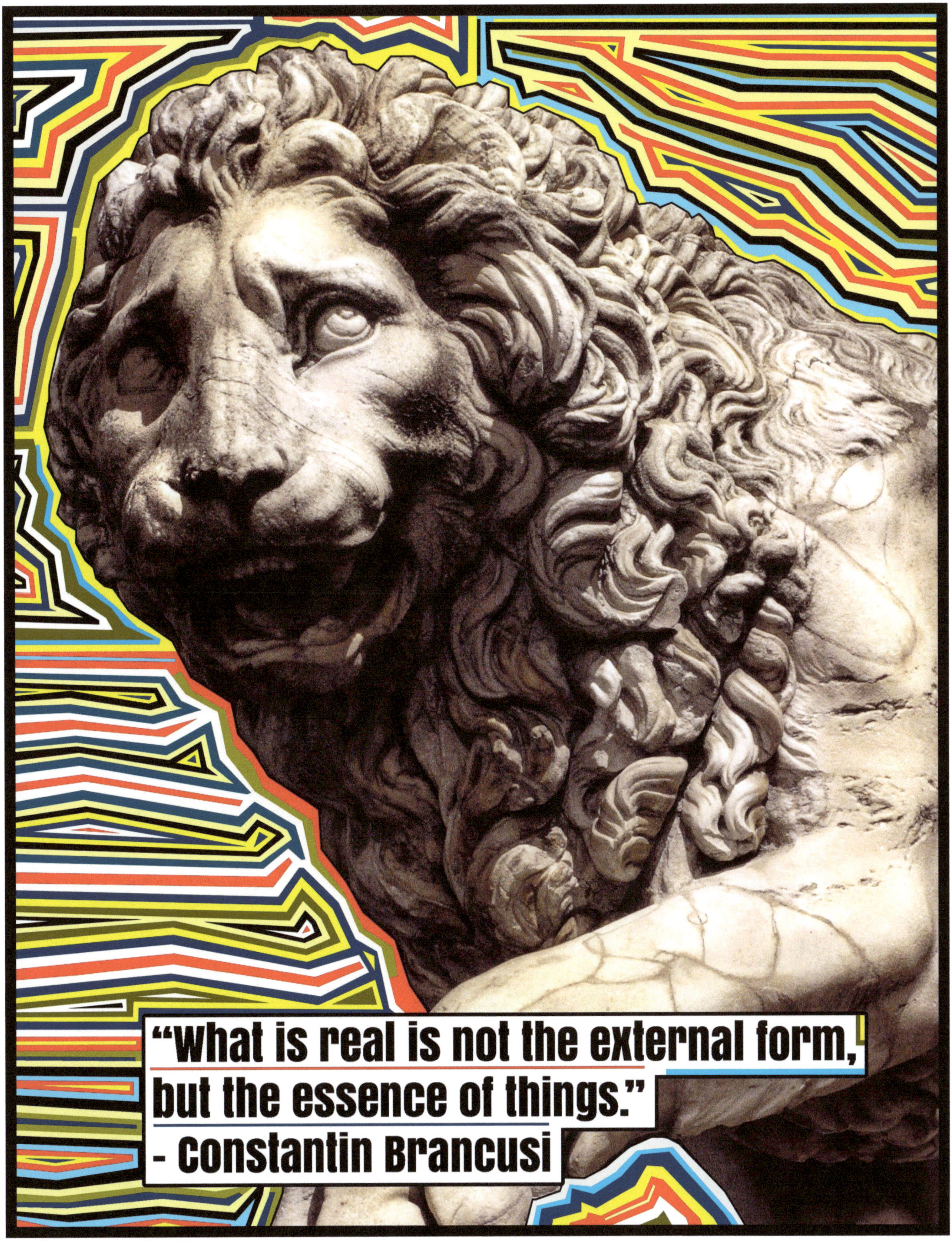
“What is real is not the external form,
but the essence of things.”
- Constantin Brancusi

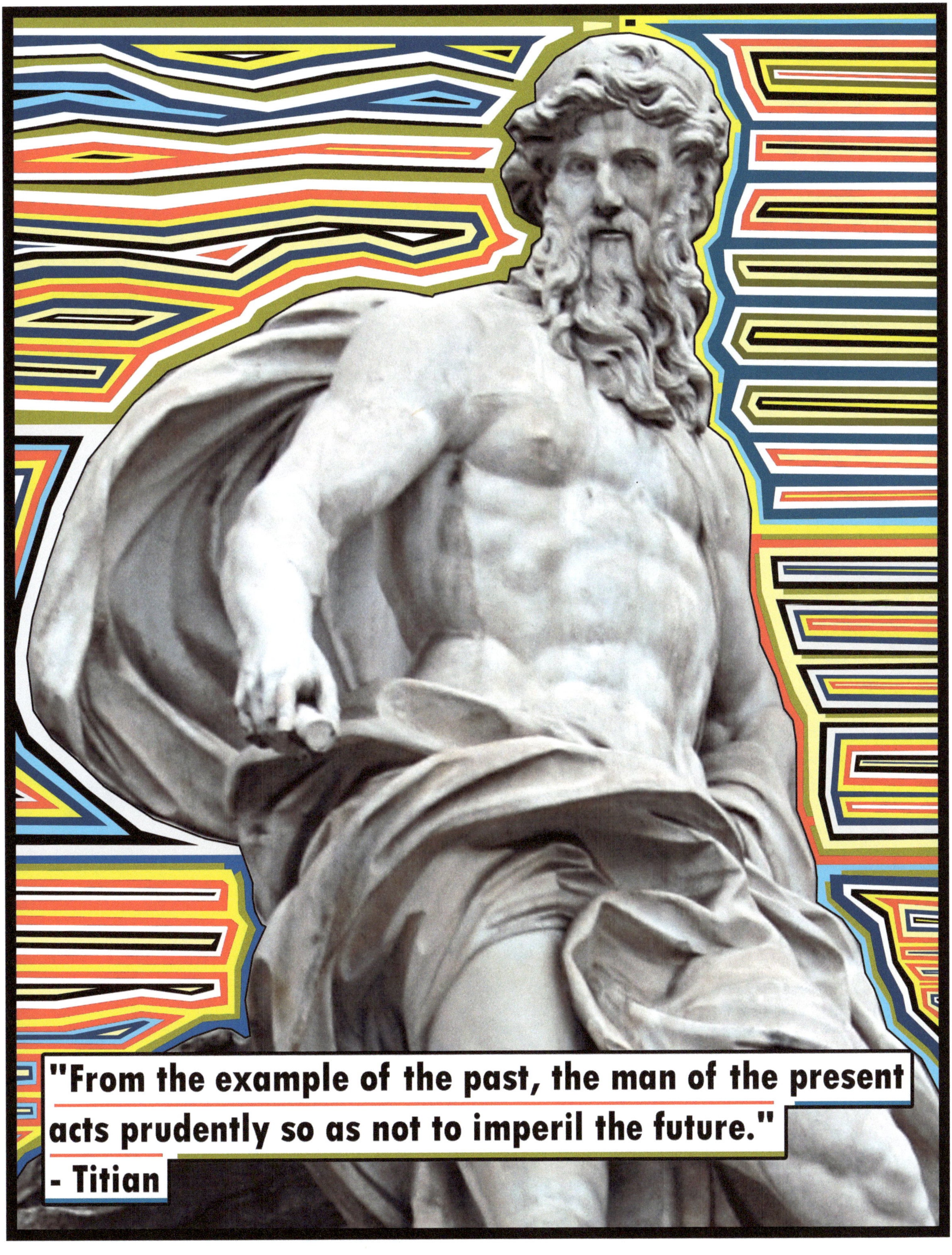
"From the example of the past, the man of the present acts prudently so as not to imperil the future."
- Titian

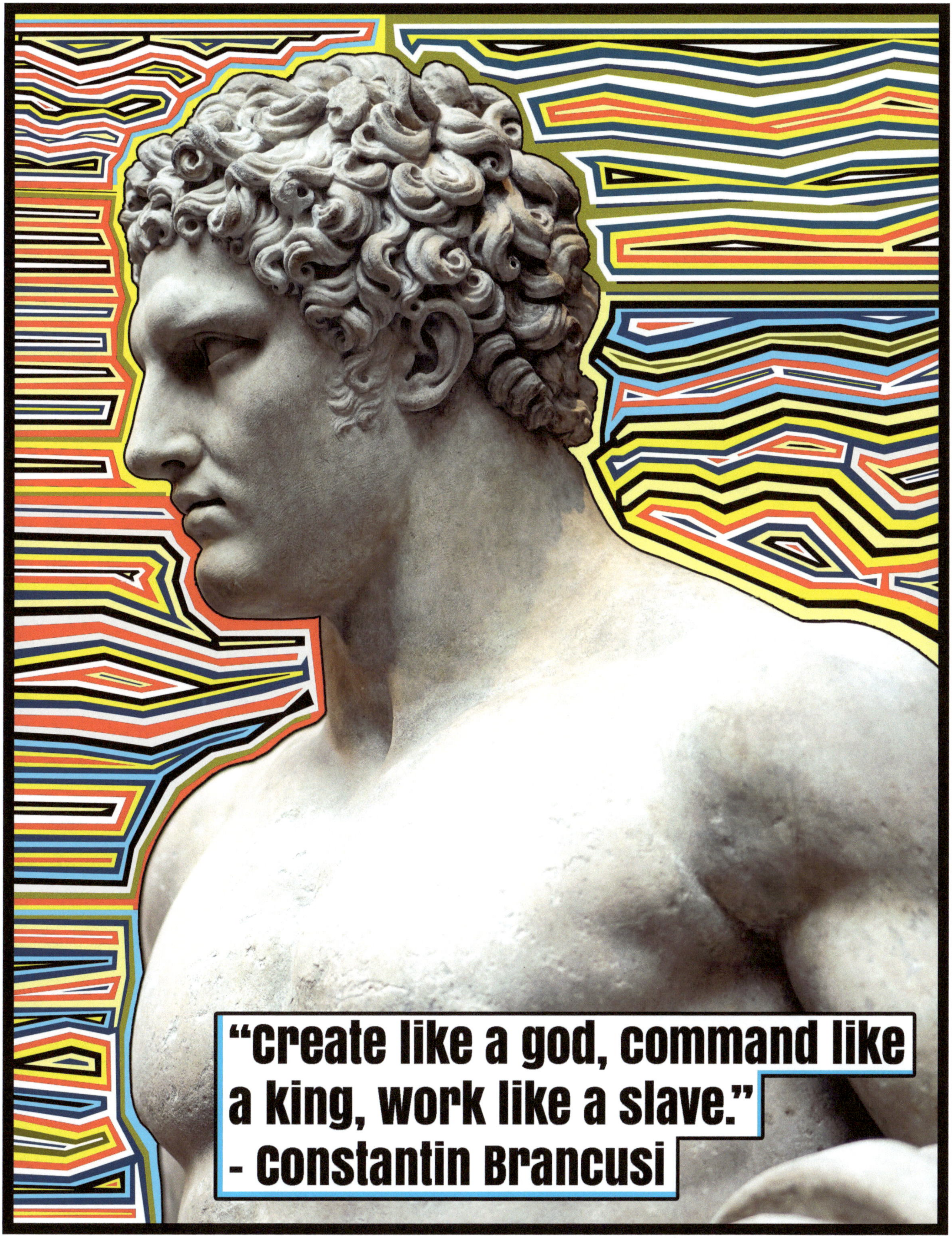
"Create like a god, command like a king, work like a slave."
- Constantin Brancusi

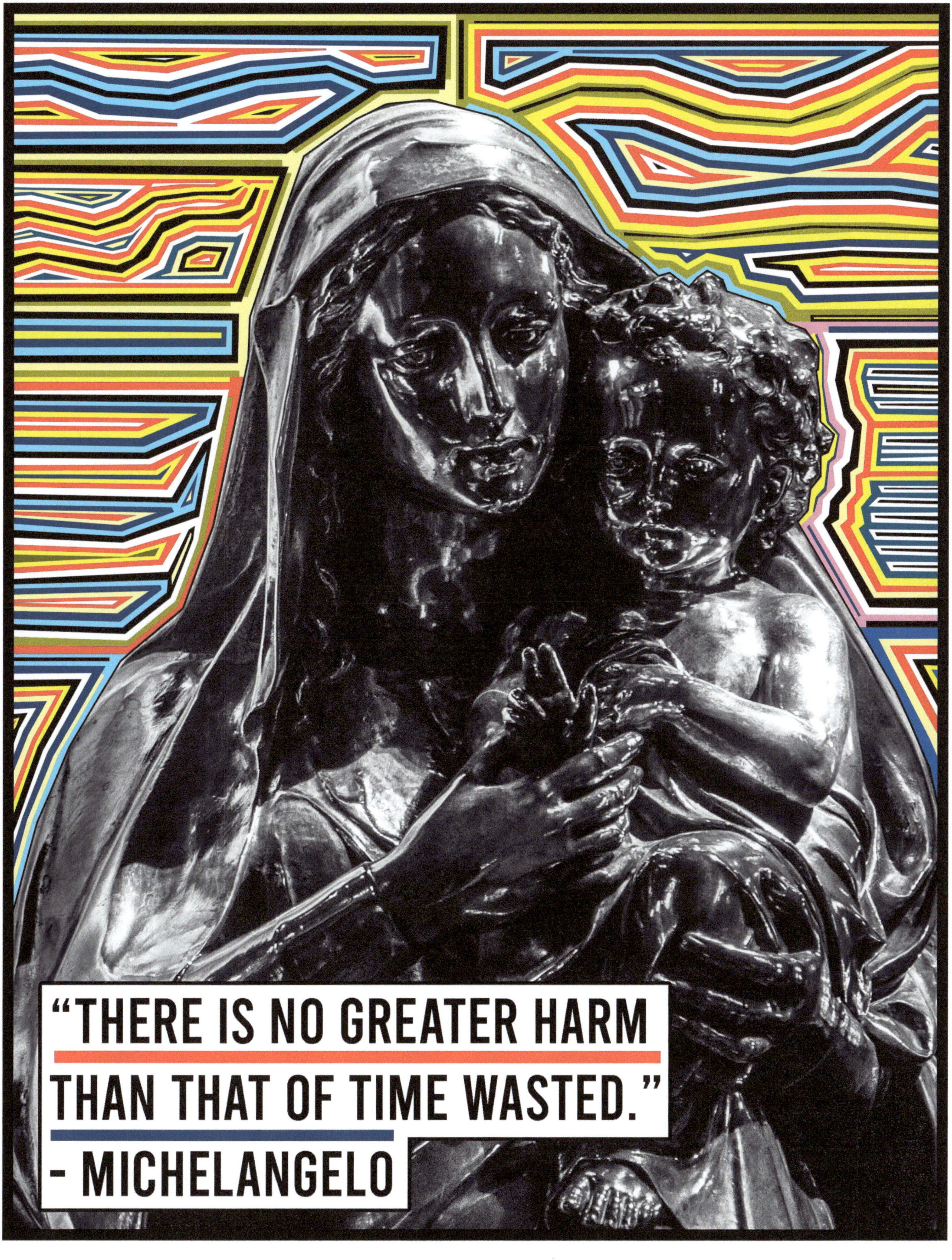
"THERE IS NO GREATER HARM
THAN THAT OF TIME WASTED."
- MICHELANGELO

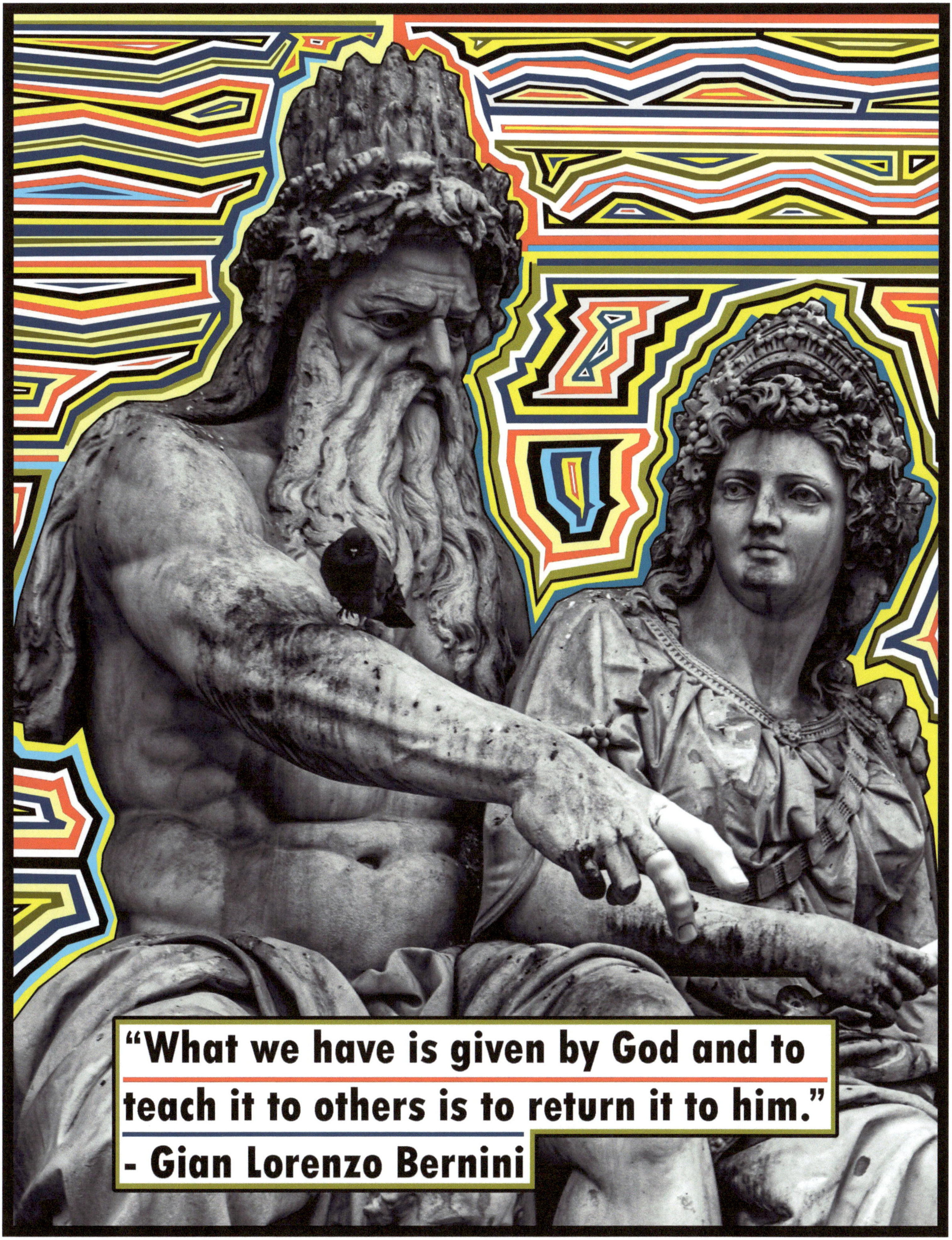
"What we have is given by God and to teach it to others is to return it to him."
- Gian Lorenzo Bernini

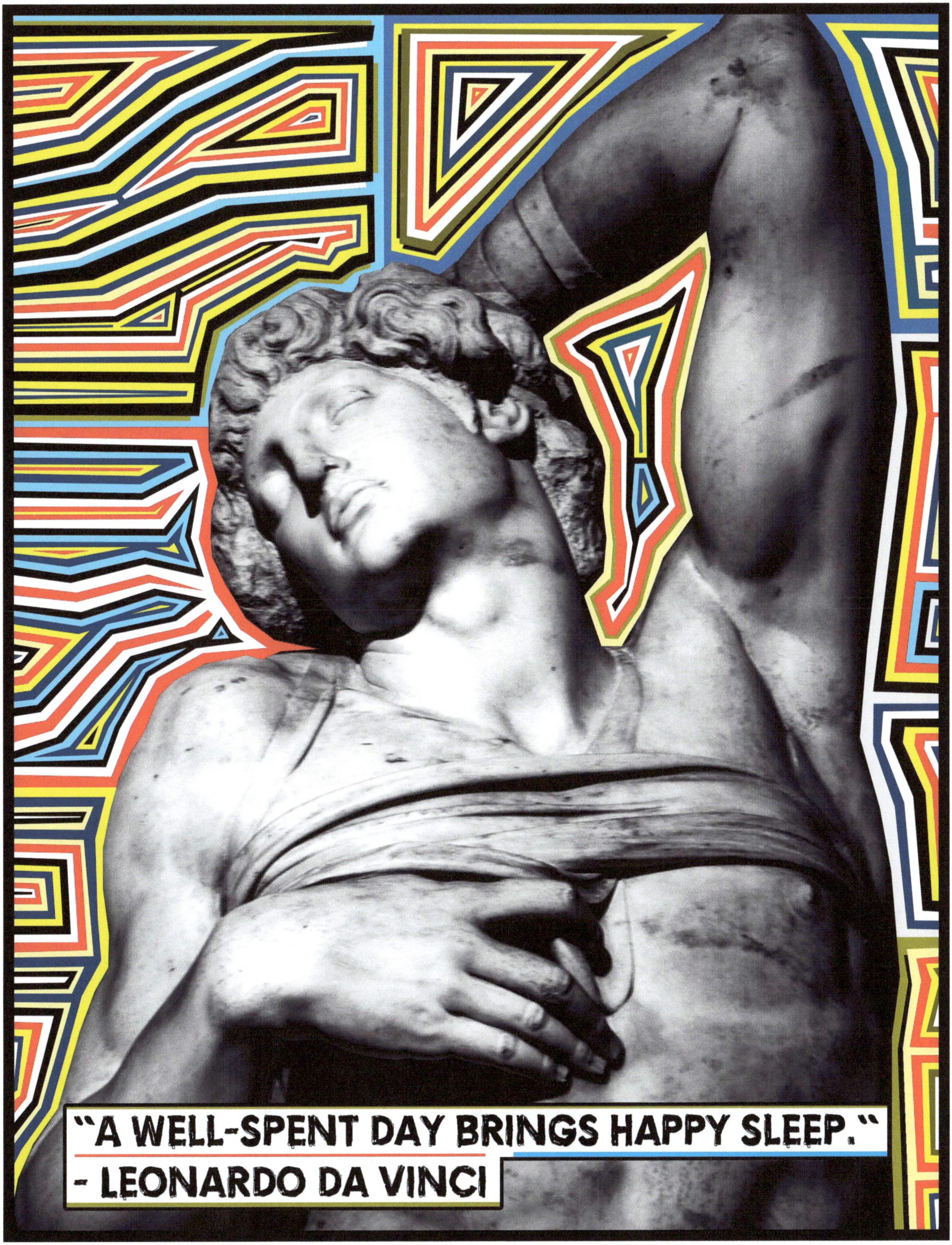
"A WELL-SPENT DAY BRINGS HAPPY SLEEP."
- LEONARDO DA VINCI

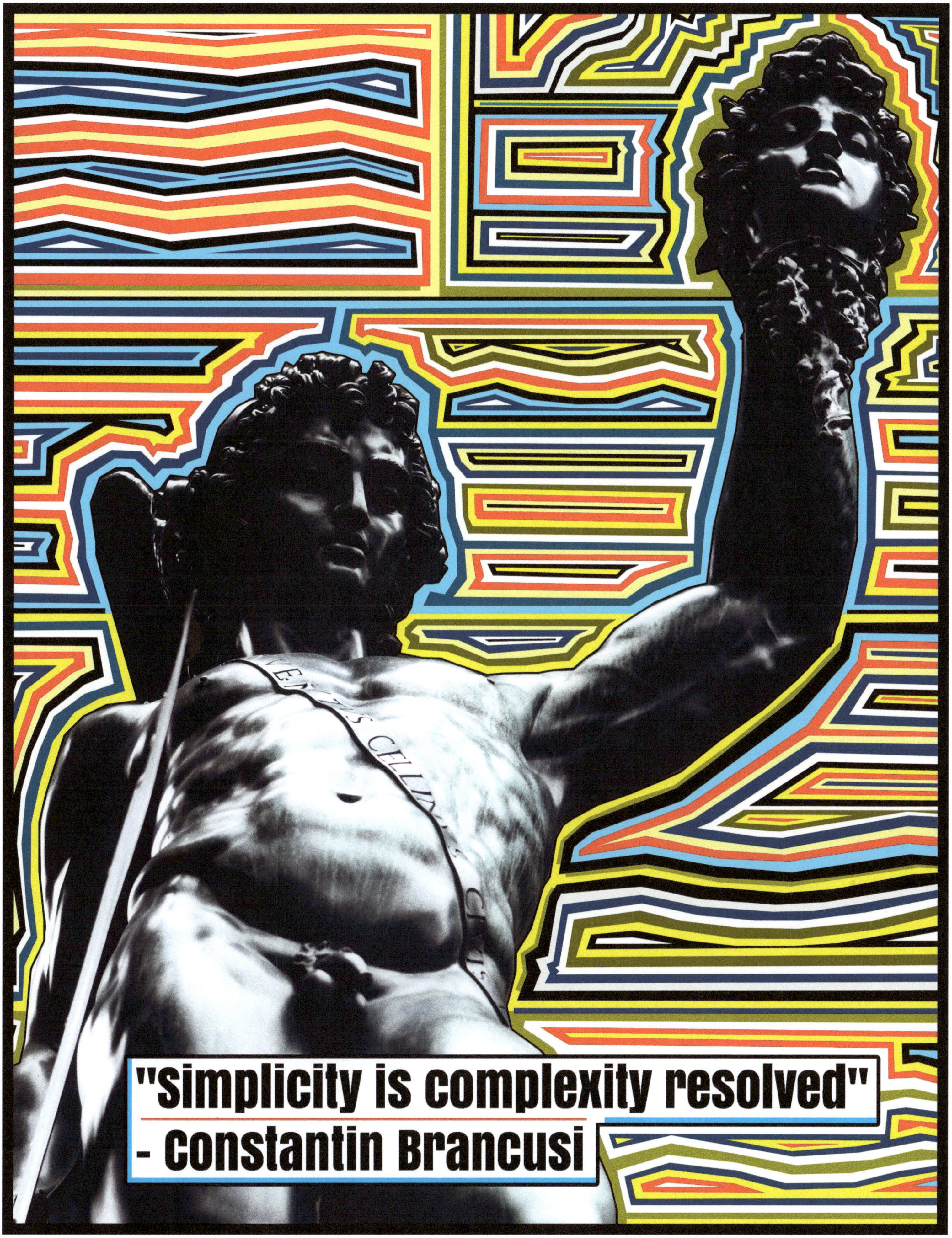
"Simplicity is complexity resolved"
- Constantin Brancusi

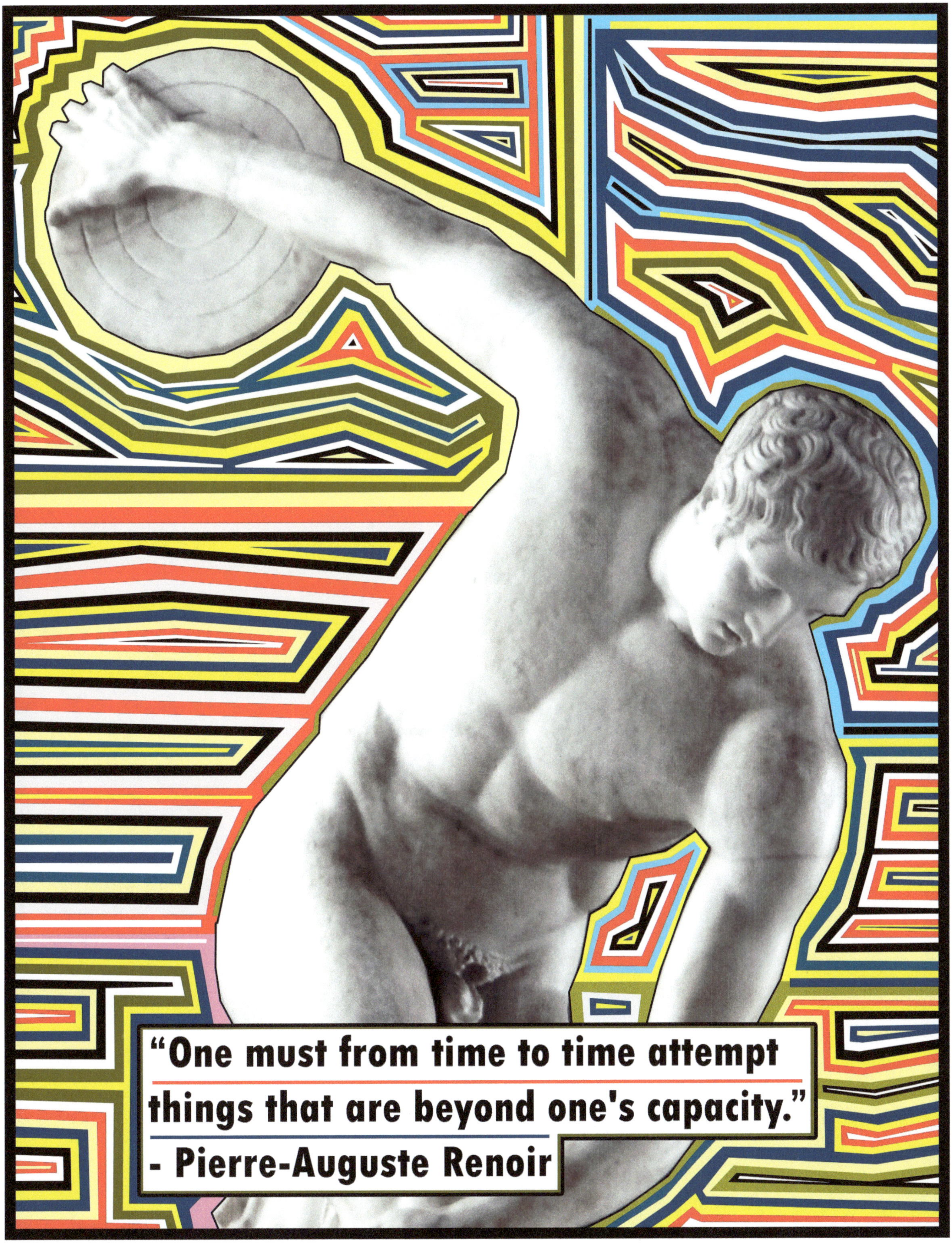
"One must from time to time attempt
things that are beyond one's capacity."
- Pierre-Auguste Renoir

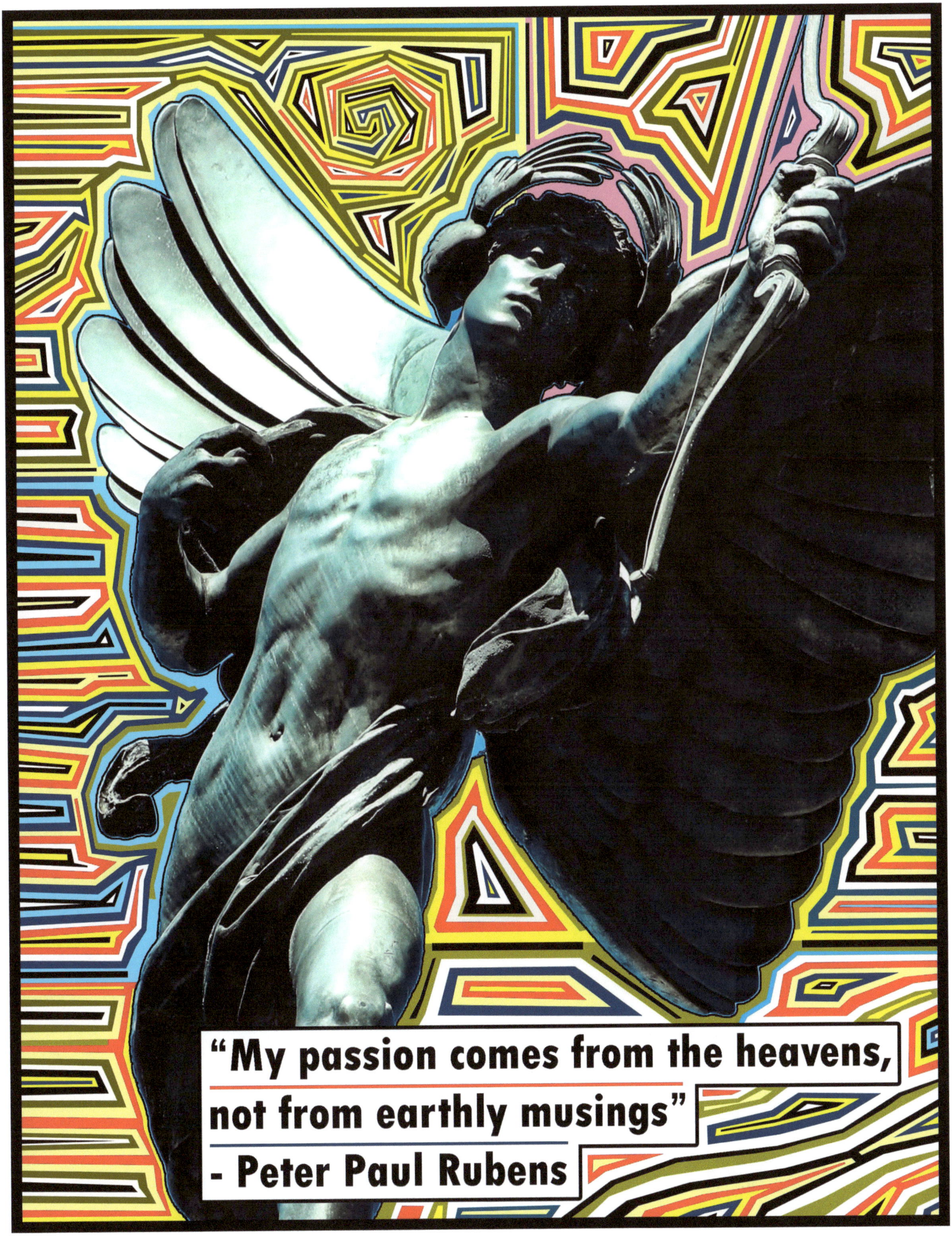
"My passion comes from the heavens,
not from earthly musings"
- Peter Paul Rubens

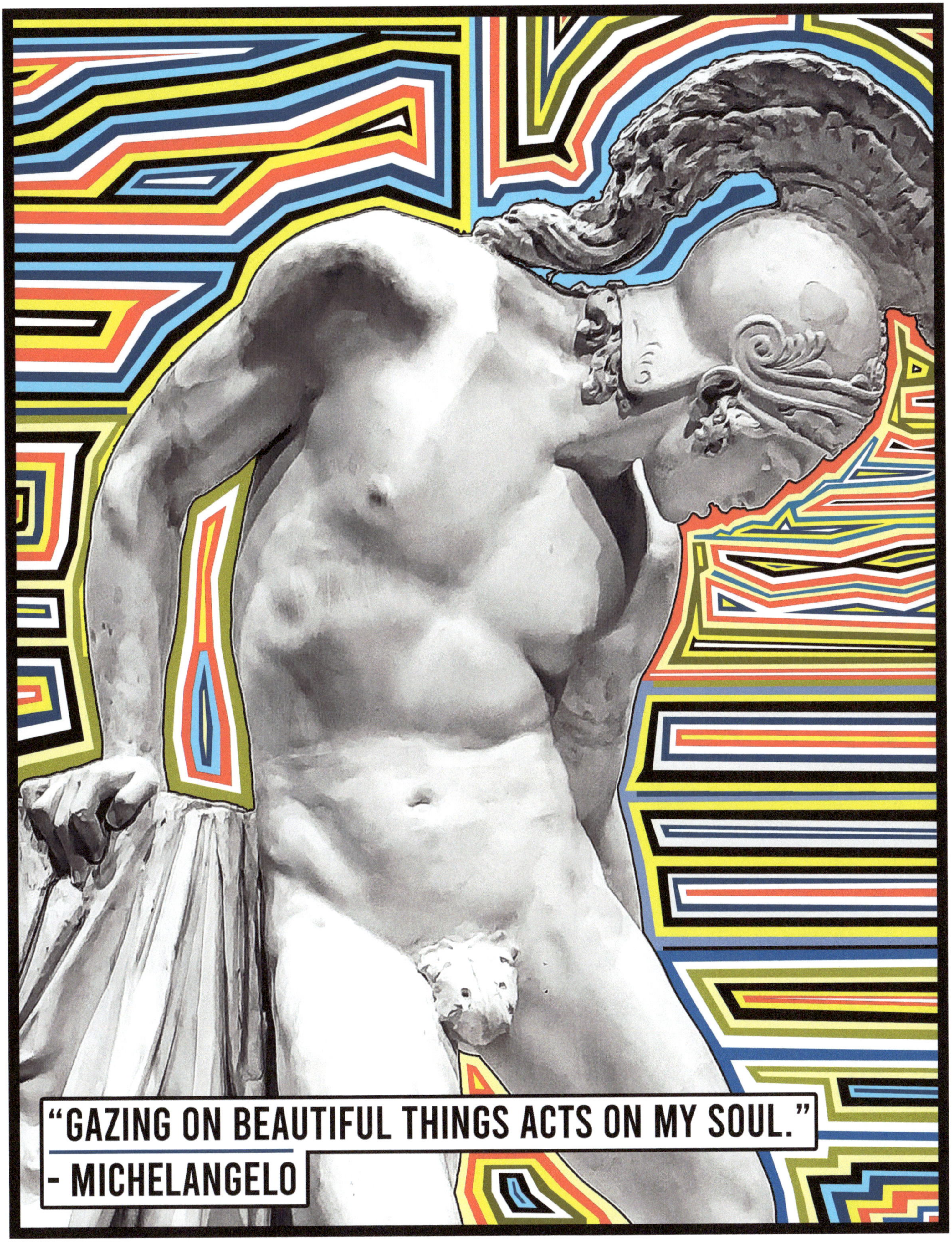
"GAZING ON BEAUTIFUL THINGS ACTS ON MY SOUL."
- MICHELANGELO

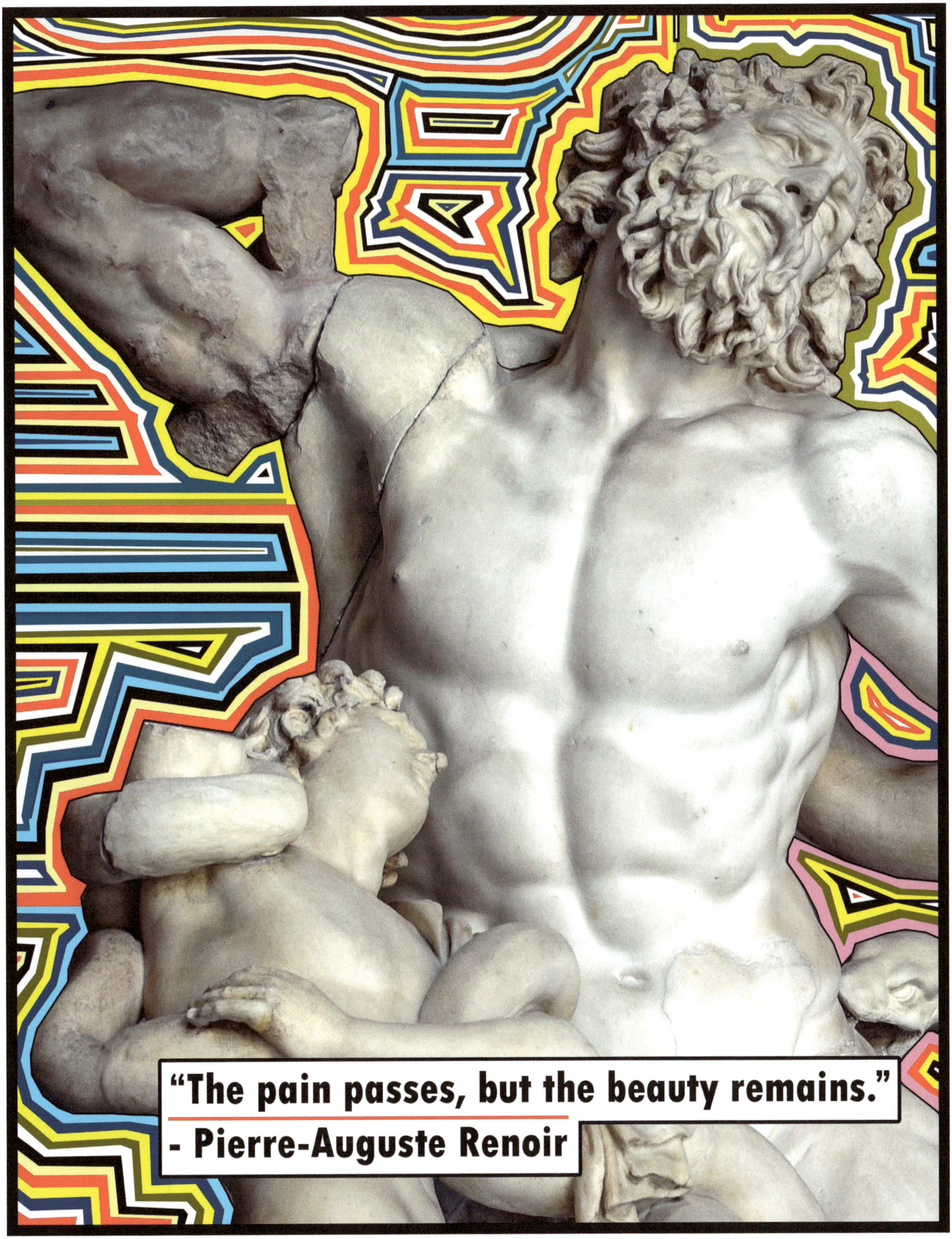
"The pain passes, but the beauty remains."
- Pierre-Auguste Renoir

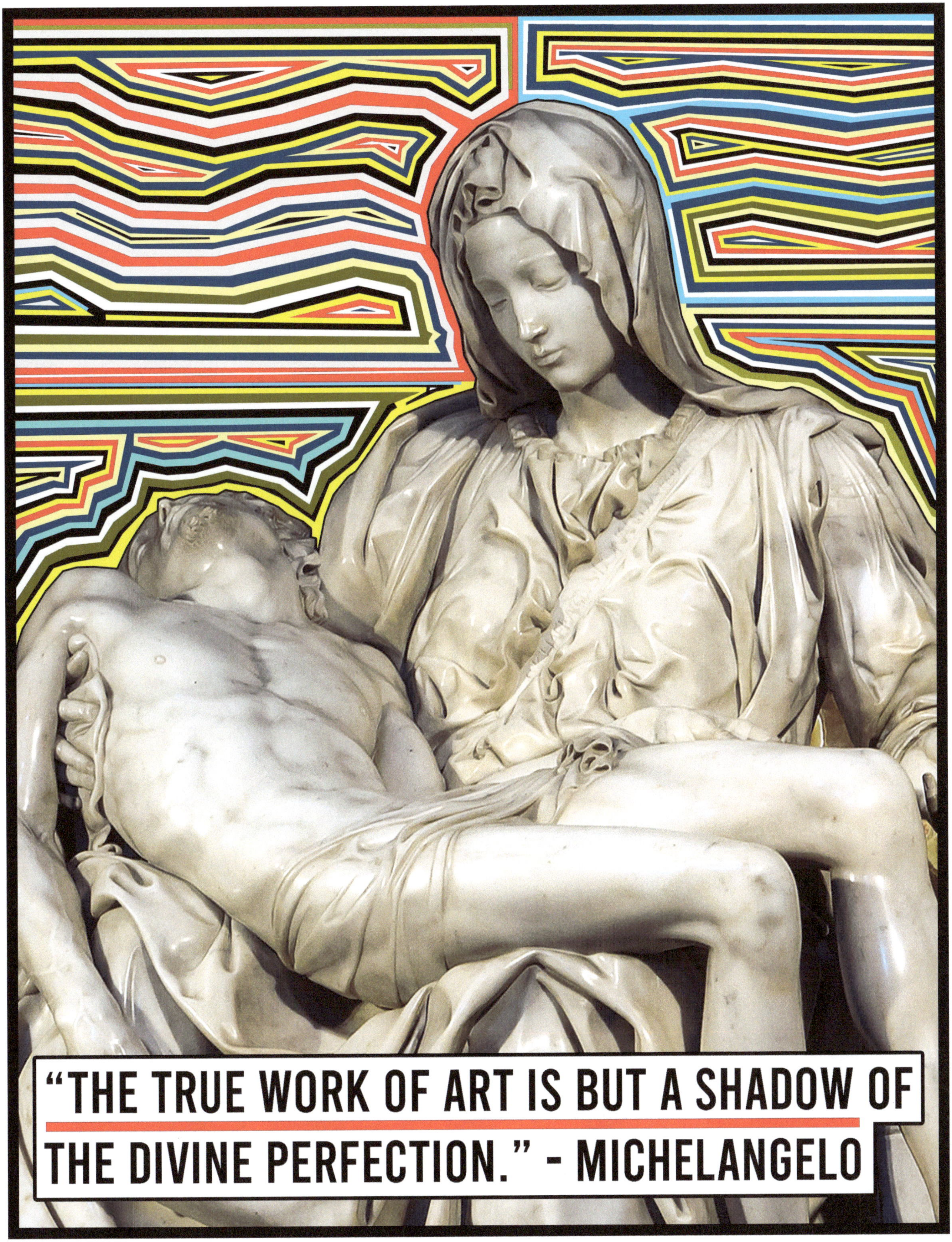
"THE TRUE WORK OF ART IS BUT A SHADOW OF
THE DIVINE PERFECTION." - MICHELANGELO

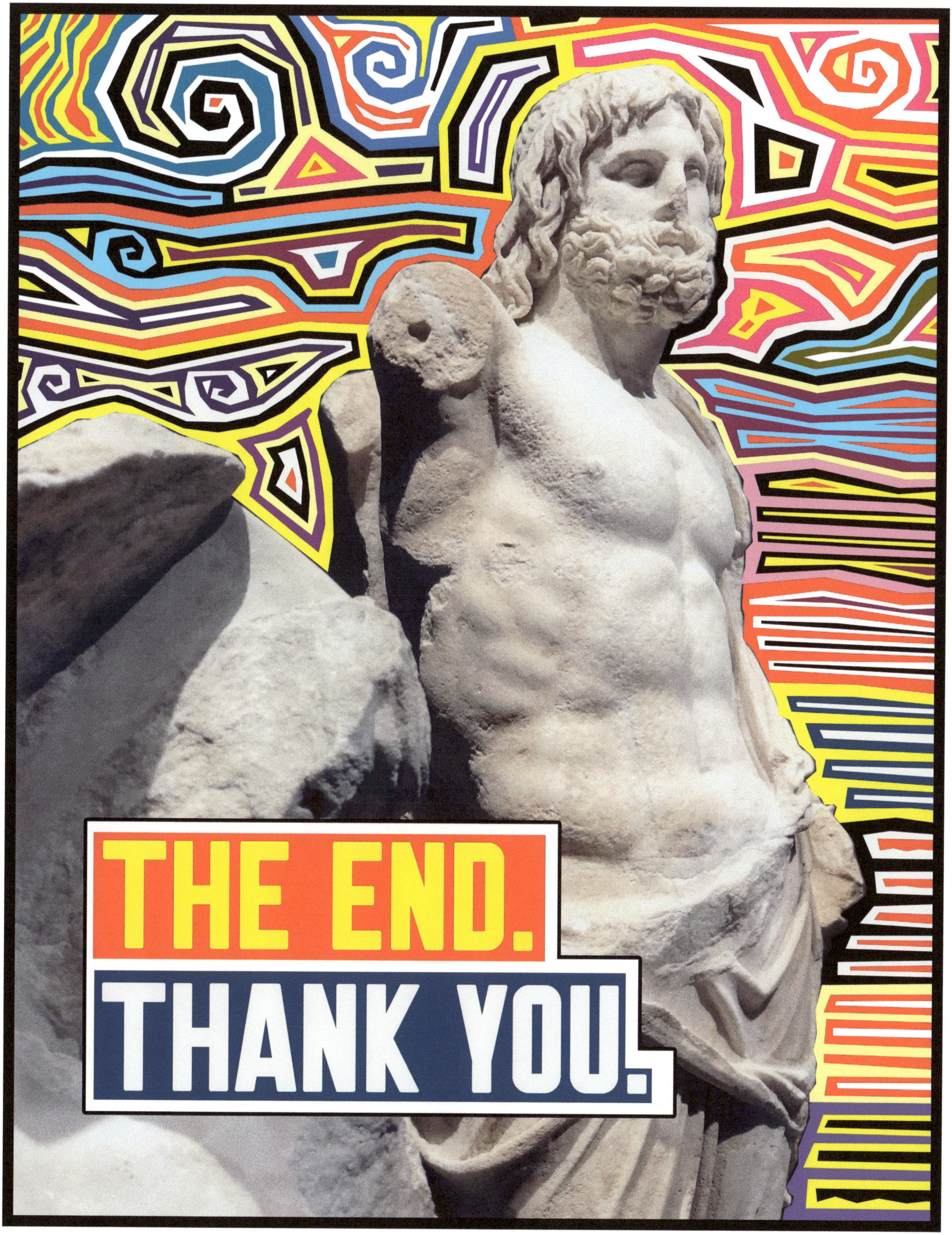
THE END.
THANK YOU.

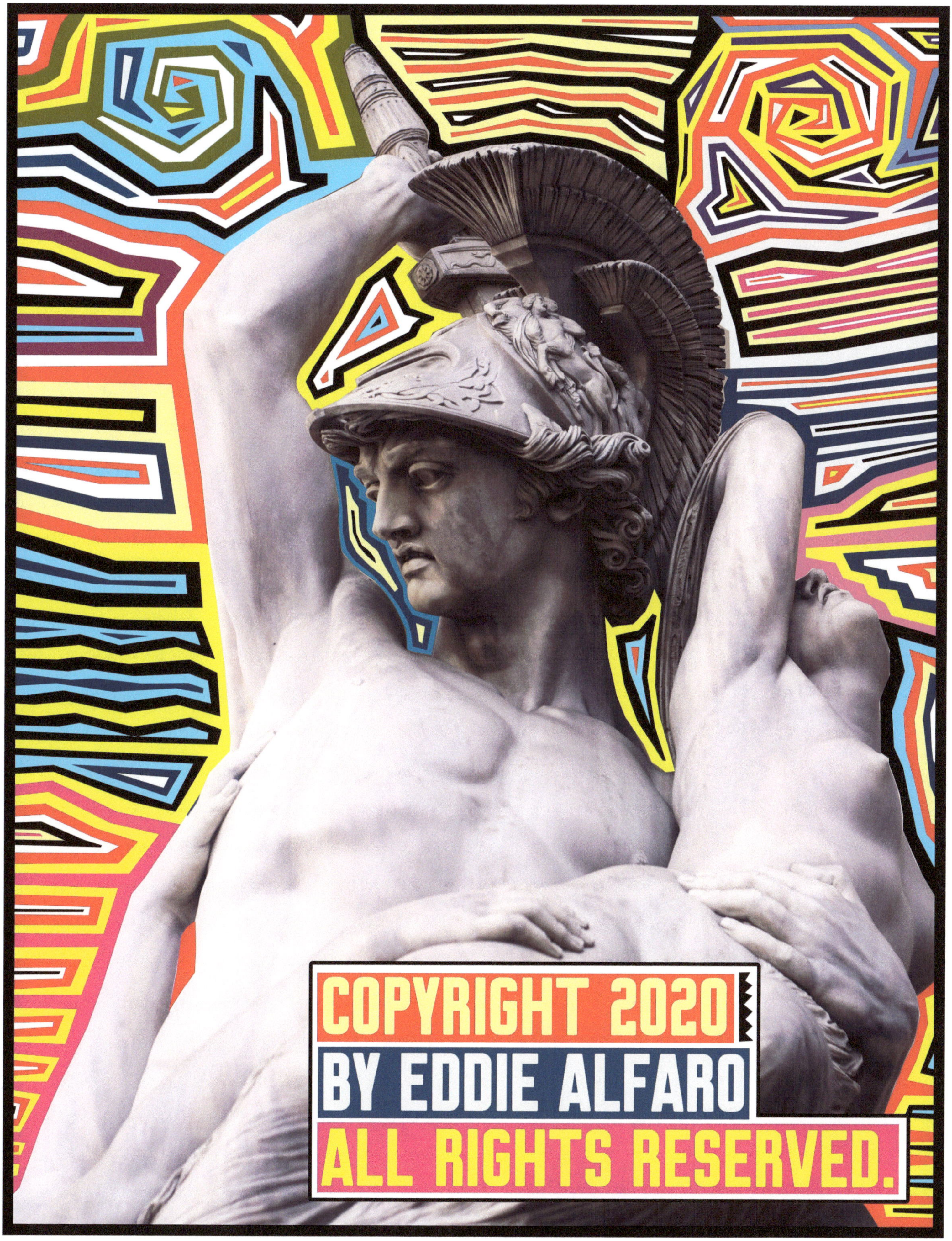
COPYRIGHT 2020
BY EDDIE ALFARO
ALL RIGHTS RESERVED.

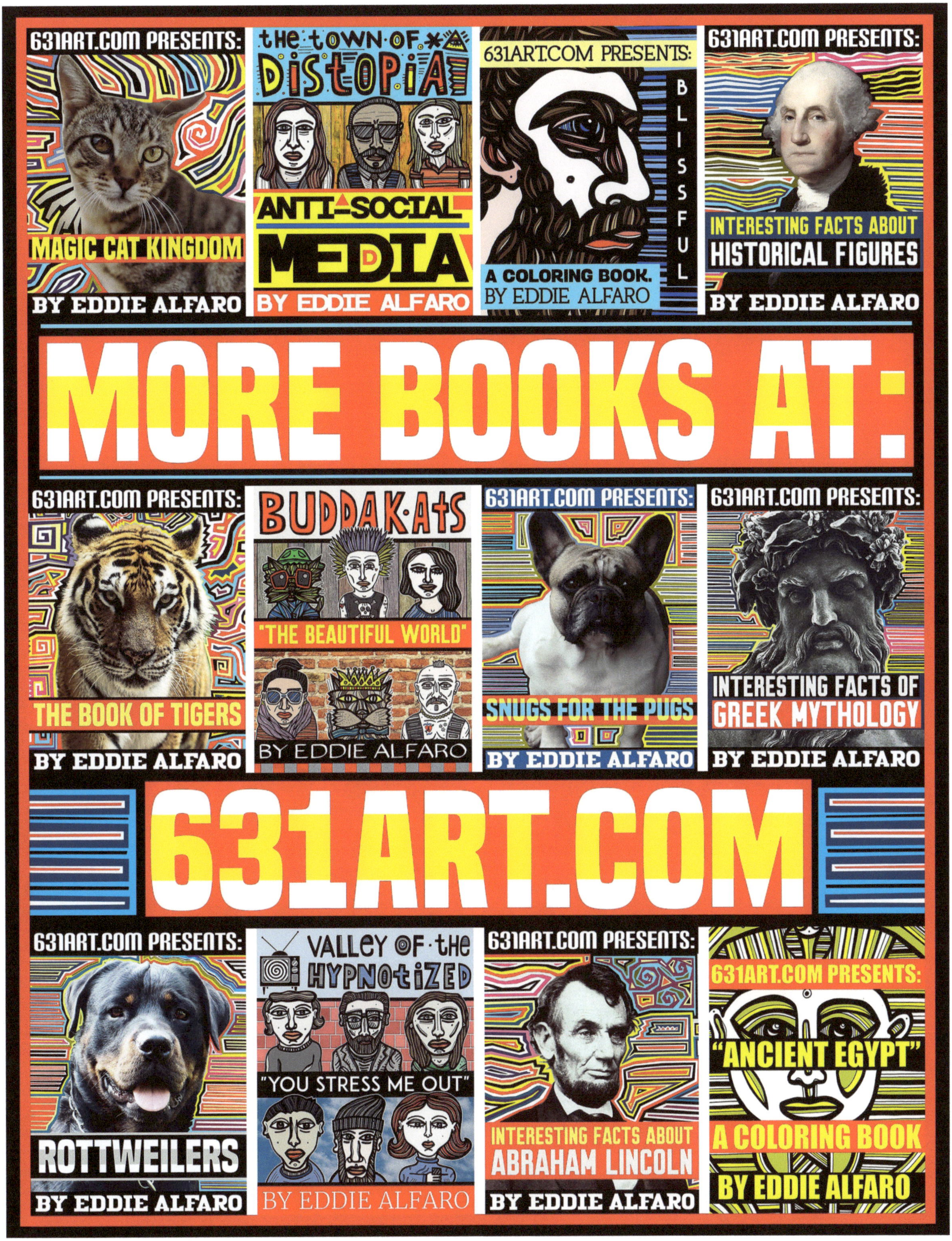
631ART.COM PRESENTS:
MAGIC CAT KINGDOM
BY EDDIE ALFARO
THE TOWN OF DISTOPIA
ANTI-SOCIAL MEDIA
BY EDDIE ALFARO
631ART.COM PRESENTS:
BLISSFUL
A COLORING BOOK.
BY EDDIE ALFARO
631ART.COM PRESENTS:
INTERESTING FACTS ABOUT
HISTORICAL FIGURES
BY EDDIE ALFARO
MORE BOOKS AT:
631ART.COM PRESENTS:
THE BOOK OF TIGERS
BY EDDIE ALFARO
BUDDAKATS
"THE BEAUTIFUL WORLD"
BY EDDIE ALFARO
631ART.COM PRESENTS:
SNUGS FOR THE PUGS
BY EDDIE ALFARO
631ART.COM PRESENTS:
INTERESTING FACTS OF
GREEK MYTHOLOGY
BY EDDIE ALFARO
631ART.COM
631ART.COM PRESENTS:
ROTTWEILERS
BY EDDIE ALFARO
VALLEY OF THE HYPNOTIZED
"YOU STRESS ME OUT"
BY EDDIE ALFARO
631ART.COM PRESENTS:
INTERESTING FACTS ABOUT
ABRAHAM LINCOLN
BY EDDIE ALFARO
631ART.COM PRESENTS:
"ANCIENT EGYPT"
A COLORING BOOK
BY EDDIE ALFARO

www.ingramcontent.com/pod-product-compliance
Lightning Source LLC
Chambersburg PA
CBHW040413220526
45473CB00004B/1227
9798712102464